Juvenile Crime

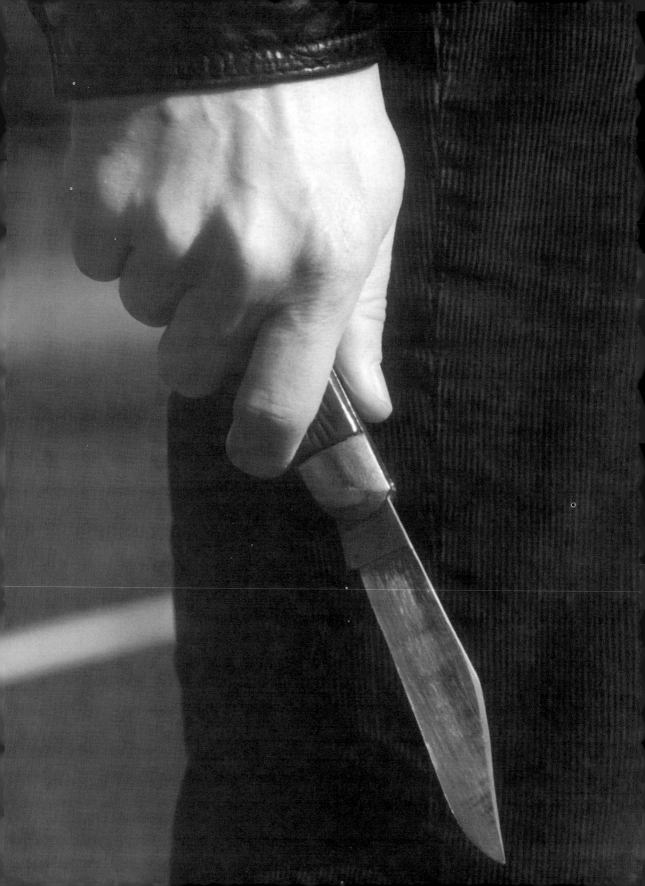

CRIME, JUSTICE, AND PUNISHMENT

Juvenile Crime

Marcia Satterthwaite

Austin Sarat, GENERAL EDITOR

CHELSEA HOUSE PUBLISHERS
Philadelphia

Chelsea House Publishers

Editor in Chief Stephen Reginald
Production Manager Pamela Loos
Art Director Sara Davis
Picture Editor Judy Hasday
Senior Production Editor Lisa Chippendale

Staff for JUVENILE CRIME

Senior Editor John Ziff
Designer Takeshi Takahashi
Picture Researcher Gillian Speeth
Cover Illustration Janet Hamlin

3 5 7 9 8 6 4

Library of Congress Cataloging-in-Publication Data

Satterthwaite, Marcia.
Juvenile crime / Marcia Satterthwaite; Austin Sarat, general editor.
   p. cm. — (Crime, justice, and punishment)
Includes bibliographical references and index.
Summary: A sociological study of the causes and rates of
crimes committed by people under eighteen years of age
and of how these offenders are handled by the justice system. Includes case histories.

ISBN 0-7910-4269-3

1. Juvenile delinquency—United States—Juvenile literature. 2. Juvenile delinquents—United States—Case studies—Juvenile literature. 3. Violent crimes—United
States—Juvenile literature. 4. Juvenile justice, Administration of—United States—Juvenile literature. [1. Juvenile
delinquency. 2. Violent crimes. 3. Justice, Administration
of.] I. Title. II. Series.
HV9104.S322 1997
364.36'0973—dc21   97-21563
                                                   CIP
                                                   AC

Contents

CRIME, JUSTICE, AND PUNISHMENT

Fears and Fascinations:

An Introduction to
Crime, Justice, and Punishment

By Austin Sarat

We live with crime and images of crime all around us. Crime evokes in most of us a deep aversion, a feeling of profound vulnerability, but it also evokes an equally deep fascination. Today, in major American cities the fear of crime is a major fact of life, some would say a disproportionate response to the realities of crime. Yet the fear of crime is real, palpable in the quickened steps and furtive glances of people walking down darkened streets. At the same time, we eagerly follow crime stories on television and in movies. We watch with a "who done it" curiosity, eager to see the illicit deed done, the investigation undertaken, the miscreant brought to justice and given his just deserts. On the streets the presence of crime is a reminder of our own vulnerability and the precariousness of our taken-for-granted rights and freedoms. On television and in the movies the crime story gives us a chance to probe our own darker motives, to ask "Is there a criminal within?" as well as to feel the collective satisfaction of seeing justice done.

Fear and fascination, these two poles of our engagement with crime, are, of course, only part of the story. Crime is, after all, a major social and legal problem, not just an issue of our individual psychology. Politicians today use our fear of, and fascination with, crime for political advantage. How we respond to crime, as well as to the political uses of the crime issue, tells us a lot about who we are as a people as well as what we value and what we tolerate. Is our response compassionate or severe? Do we seek to understand or to punish, to enact an angry vengeance or to rehabilitate and welcome the criminal back into our midst? The CRIME, JUSTICE, AND PUNISHMENT series is designed to explore these themes, to ask why we are fearful and fascinated, to probe the meanings and motivations of crimes and criminals and of our responses to them, and, finally, to ask what we can learn about ourselves and the society in which we live by examining our responses to crime.

Crime is always a challenge to the prevailing normative order and a test of the values and commitments of law-abiding people. It is sometimes a Raskolnikov-like act of defiance, an assertion of the unwillingness of some to live according to the rules of conduct laid out by organized society. In this sense, crime marks the limits of the law and reminds us of law's all-too-regular failures. Yet sometimes there is more desperation than defiance in criminal acts; sometimes they signal a deep pathology or need in the criminal. To confront crime is thus also to come face-to-face with the reality of social difference, of class privilege and extreme deprivation, of race and racism, of children neglected, abandoned, or abused whose response is to enact on others what they have experienced themselves. And occasionally crime, or what is labeled a criminal act, represents a call for justice, an appeal to a higher moral order against the inadequacies of existing law.

Figuring out the meaning of crime and the motivations of criminals and whether crime arises from defiance, desperation, or the appeal for justice is never an easy task. The motivations and meanings of crime are as varied as are the persons who engage in criminal conduct. They are as mysterious as any of the mysteries of the human soul. Yet the desire to know the secrets of crime and the criminal is a strong one, for in that knowledge may lie one step on the road to protection, if not an assurance of one's own personal safety. Nonetheless, as strong as that desire may be, there is no available technology that can allow us to know the whys of crime with much confidence, let alone a scientific certainty. We can, however, capture something about crime by studying the defiance, desperation, and quest for justice that may be associated with it. Books in the CRIME, JUSTICE, AND PUNISHMENT series will take up that challenge. They tell stories of crime and criminals, some famous, most not, some glamorous and exciting, most mundane and commonplace.

This series will, in addition, take a sober look at American criminal justice, at the procedures through which we investigate crimes and identify criminals, at the institutions in which innocence or guilt is determined. In these procedures and institutions we confront the thrill of the chase as well as the challenge of protecting the rights of those who defy our laws. It is through the efficiency and dedication of law enforcement that we might capture the criminal; it is in the rare instances of their corruption or brutality that we feel perhaps our deepest betrayal. Police, prosecutors, defense lawyers, judges, and jurors administer criminal justice and in their daily actions give substance to the guarantees of the Bill of Rights. What is an adversarial system of justice? How does it work? Why do we have it? Books in the CRIME, JUSTICE, AND PUNISHMENT series will examine the thrill of the chase as we seek to capture the criminal. They will also reveal the drama and majesty of the criminal trial as well as the day-to-day reality of a criminal justice system in which trials are the exception and negotiated pleas of guilty are the rule.

When the trial is over or the plea has been entered, when we have separated the innocent from the guilty, the moment of punishment has arrived. The injunction to punish the guilty, to respond to pain inflicted by inflicting pain, is as old as civilization itself. "An eye for an eye and a tooth for a tooth" is a biblical reminder that punishment must measure pain for pain. But our response to the criminal must be better than and different from the crime itself. The biblical admonition, along with the constitutional prohibition of "cruel and unusual punishment," signals that we seek to punish justly and to be just not only in the determination of who can and should be punished, but in how we punish as well. But neither reminder tells us what to do with the wrongdoer. Do we rape the rapist, or burn the home of the arsonist? Surely justice and decency say no. But, if not, then how can and should we punish? In a world in which punishment is neither identical to the crime nor an automatic response to it, choices must be made and we must make them. Books in the CRIME, JUSTICE, AND PUNISHMENT series will examine those choices and the practices, and politics, of punishment. How do we punish and why do we punish as we do? What can we learn about the rationality and appropriateness of today's responses to crime by examining our past and its responses? What works? Is there, and can there be, a just measure of pain?

CRIME, JUSTICE, AND PUNISHMENT brings together books on some of the great themes of human social life. The books in this series capture our fear and fascination with crime and examine our responses to it. They remind us of the deadly seriousness of these subjects. They bring together themes in law, literature, and popular culture to challenge us to think again, to think anew, about subjects that go to the heart of who we are and how we can and will live together.

*   *   *   *   *

All crime, particularly when it involves violence, is shocking. Juvenile crime is especially shocking. The image of childhood as the age of innocence, which pervades our culture, means that most of us are unprepared for crime by kids. We do not know how to react. Should we give juvenile criminals a break and treat them with a forgiving compassion? Alternatively, should we react severely, with a strictness that might bring them to their senses? Historically, the treatment of juvenile offenders moved in the direction of leniency; we called them delinquents rather than criminals in the hope that the kinder label would stir them in the right direction. Now, severity is the order of the day. As a society we have given up hope that we can, through acts of compassion, redeem juveniles who engage in adult-like lawlessness. The image of childhood innocence has given way to the image of the predatory street thug.

Juvenile Crime tells the story of this historical transformation. It does so by exploring the antecedents of today's juvenile justice policies, including the origins of the juvenile court. This book presents a vivid and compelling picture of why juveniles commit the crimes they do and what happens to them in their encounter with the legal system. Seen from the perspective of kids in trouble with the law, *Juvenile Crime* conveys the complexity of the juvenile crime problem. Should juveniles be sent to adult prisons? Are kids better bets for rehabilitation than adult criminals? Can kids be helped through therapeutic intervention? Can our society afford to provide such help even if it seems warranted? Should kids who kill be subject to capital punishment? Each of these issues is addressed with clarity and insight. In the end, *Juvenile Crime* presents a comprehensive, though readable, account, taking us behind the headlines that grab our attention so that we can develop a deep understanding of a significant national problem.

THE RISING TIDE OF YOUTH VIOLENCE

B y the time he pulled the trigger, 15-year-old Terrance had stopped thinking. For weeks a group of kids led by the oldest, Joe, had been waiting for him every afternoon when the school bus dropped him off at the bottom of the hill. From the stoop of Joe's house they would hurl insults at Terrance as he walked up the steep street toward his aunt's home. The insults were of the typical adolescent variety— taunts about Terrance's intelligence, his manhood, his clothes—but they were constant.

Initially Terrance had fired back some insults and threats of his own, but this only seemed to make the boys louder and more abusive. One day he decided to ignore his tormentors and walk, eyes fixed on the pavement, past Joe's house. But Joe followed him halfway up the block, sneering taunts and challenges while the others urged him on. This escalation had prompted

An all-too-common American street scene: the violent end of a young life.

Terrance to turn and fight, and although he had gotten the better of the encounter, he found Joe in his accustomed place the next afternoon, leading his boys in their chorus of insults.

The day Joe brought up Terrance's younger sister, Arielle, proved to be the turning point. Terrance had always considered himself Arielle's protector, especially during the last four years, when they'd been shuffled from relative to relative following their mother's third drug arrest. So when Joe shouted that Arielle had

At play in the inner city. Poverty and community disorganization contribute to a child's risk of delinquency and violence, experts believe.

performed a certain sex act for him, Terrance couldn't let that disrespect go. He was already well past Joe's house when he heard the words. Stopping in his tracks, he wheeled around and took a few quick steps down the hill. Then he got a better idea. Slowly he turned and proceeded up the hill, the sound of laughter and jeers ringing in his ears.

At home, while Aunt Wanda was downstairs in the kitchen, Terrance went into her bedroom and removed the shoe box from the top shelf of the bedroom closet. In it, he knew, was the handgun Aunt Wanda's boyfriend had given her for protection.

The next afternoon, as the bus pulled away, Terrance unzipped his backpack and rooted around for the T-shirt he had used to wrap the gun. He unfurled it and, holding the backpack in front of him to conceal the gun he now held in his right hand, Terrance calmly walked up the hill. As he neared Joe's house, Joe casually rose to his feet and began launching his first insults.

What happened next seemed to Terrance to unfold in slow motion, almost as if it were a dream in which he played no part. The backpack fell to the ground, Terrance's hand leveled the gun at Joe, and a single shot rang out.

With that act Terrance became part of an alarming national trend: the rising tide of violence committed by kids, arguably the most conspicuous aspect of today's debate about juvenile crime in America.

The causes of juvenile crime and violence are complex. According to the federal Office of Juvenile Justice and Delinquency Prevention,

> There is no single cause of delinquency and violence. Delinquents, especially chronic delinquents, exhibit a variety of social and psychological deficits in their backgrounds. These deficits, often referred to as risk factors, stem from breakdowns in five influential domains in juveniles' lives: neighborhood, family, school, peers, and individual characteristics.

Risk factors, such as community disorganization, availability of drugs and firearms, and persistent poverty, make children more prone to involvement in delinquent behavior than if those factors were not present. Additionally, when a child's family life is filled with violence, problem behaviors, poor parental monitoring, and inconsistent disciplinary practices or maltreatment, a child's risk of delinquency increases. Youth exhibiting combinations of deficits in multiple domains of their lives are at highest risk of delinquency.

Because many of the risk factors—poverty, readily available drugs, inadequate schools, and dangerous, decaying neighborhoods—are concentrated in the inner city, kids there are at increased risk for crime and violence. Juvenile arrest rates for violent crime are about twice as high in cities as in suburban counties, for example. But the view of juvenile crime and violence as predominantly an urban problem is mistaken. Drugs, guns, child abuse, and dysfunctional families are present virtually everywhere in the United States, and for that reason no community is immune from the problem of young lawbreakers.

Violence pervades American culture, affecting people at all levels of society. Our murder rate, for example, is among the highest in the world, more than 15 times that of England and 20 times that of Japan. But while the overall rate of violent crime in the United States has recently declined, the rate for juveniles—those under the age of 18—appears to be on the rise. In the five-year period from 1990 to 1994, violent offenses among juveniles increased by 68 percent. In 1995 law enforcement agencies made 115,592 arrests of juveniles for violent crimes, according to the Uniform Crime Report compiled by the Federal Bureau of Investigation (FBI). Among these were 2,560 homicide arrests.

Beyond the increase in numbers, some observers have noted a disturbing change in the nature of the crimes and of the kids who commit them. On the whole, they believe, the crimes are more vicious and senseless than, say, those committed by juveniles 20 years ago. And the offenders are getting younger and more cavalier.

Terrance, only 15 years old, used deadly force because, as he told a police officer after his arrest, Joe had crossed the line by "disrespecting" him and his sister Arielle. Verbal sparring, harsh but of a kind adolescent males have engaged in for generations, became a reason to kill. And yet, disturbing as it is to contemplate a murder committed by a person not even old enough to drive a car, many Americans wouldn't consider Terrance's crime overly shocking. Perhaps this is a measure of how violent our society has become. Perhaps it's because both the killer and the victim were African Americans and the crime occurred in a poor urban area, where we expect violence to take place. Or perhaps it's because years of media accounts have inured us to all but the most senseless, vicious, and

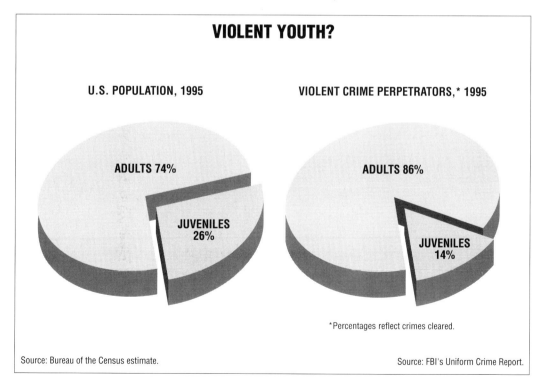

VIOLENT YOUTH?

U.S. POPULATION, 1995

ADULTS 74%

JUVENILES 26%

VIOLENT CRIME PERPETRATORS,* 1995

ADULTS 86%

JUVENILES 14%

*Percentages reflect crimes cleared.

Source: Bureau of the Census estimate.

Source: FBI's Uniform Crime Report.

Michael Ponkraskow (right) smiles for the cameras, February 15, 1927. The 11-year-old had just been apprehended for the murder of a shopkeeper. While we associate such chilling behavior with today's "epidemic" of conscienceless young killers, that epidemic, some observers contend, is merely an illusion created by disproportionate media coverage of the most senseless and brutal juvenile crimes.

unprovoked of juvenile crimes—and there was, after all, a certain degree of provocation in Terrance's case.

Other cases—the truly headline-producing ones—have caused millions of Americans to wonder whether something has gone terribly wrong with a substantial segment of today's youth. Consider, for example, the following. In Chicago, an 11-year-old boy on probation for armed robbery murdered a 14-year-old girl—just to win the respect of gang members. In rural Ohio, a $2^{1}/_{2}$-year-old girl was murdered by two boys—ages 6 and 10.

In Detroit, police arrested a 14-year-old who was calmly eating dinner only hours after he had executed another 14-year-old by shooting him point blank in the head. In New York City, a pack of teenage boys attacked a female jogger in Central Park, beating her unconscious, gang-raping her, and leaving her for dead.

Do cases such as these represent rare occurrences that are given undue attention in the media, thus skewing public perceptions of America's youth crime problem? Or are juvenile offenders today really different—more callous, more dangerous, more preda-

CRIME AND CRIME STATISTICS

Crime statistics aren't always straightforward and have been used to bolster a variety of views. Many factors contribute to crime rates, and separating the causes of a particular trend from incidental factors can be tricky. Short-term fluctuations in crime rates may or may not have much relevance, and even assessments of how many crimes have been committed over a given period vary with the methodologies used to collect the statistics.

Two of the primary sources experts rely on to provide a statistical picture of crime in the United States are the Uniform Crime Report and the National Crime Victimization Survey. The Uniform Crime Report, produced each year by the FBI, is a compilation of crime and arrest figures from local jurisdictions throughout the country. Trends are tracked through the Crime Index, which is composed of eight selected offenses, called "index crimes," in two categories: violent crimes and property crimes. The four offenses in the violent crime category are murder and nonnegligent manslaughter, forcible rape, robbery, and aggravated assault. The index property crimes are burglary, larceny-theft, motor vehicle theft, and arson.

Not all crimes show up in the Uniform Crime Report, however, because not all jurisdictions contribute data to the FBI and because a sizable number of crimes are never reported to the police. The National Crime Victimization Survey is designed to fill in these gaps. Produced annually by the U.S. Justice Department's Bureau of Justice Statistics, it is based on interviews with thousands of scientifically selected households, who report whether and how often they have been criminally victimized during the year, as well as what the particular crimes were. Like a well-designed market research survey or public opinion poll, the Justice Department's survey allows statisticians to extrapolate, from the responses of a relatively small sample, how many Americans have been victimized and how many crimes have been committed during the year. The survey doesn't, however, capture information about crimes against children under 12.

Do arrest statistics distort the scope of violent juvenile crime? Yes, some experts argue, because kids tend to commit crimes in groups and police departments tend to round up groups of juveniles when a crime has been committed.

tory—than ever before? Are we in the midst of or on the verge of an explosion in violent juvenile crime, or are current crime rates comparable to rates in the past after demographic and other factors are considered?

Experts disagree on the answers to these key questions. On one side are those who insist that the juvenile crime crisis is real and will likely get even worse. Among the most prominent of this group is John J. DiIulio, a Princeton University professor of politics and public affairs who coined the term *super-predator* to describe what he believes is an evolving new breed of juvenile criminal whose propensity for violence without remorse has reached unparalleled heights. In a 1995 article in the conservative *Weekly Standard*, DiIulio linked the origins of the nation's emerging super-predators with the disintegration of America's traditional social fabric. Raised in a world of "abject moral poverty," these children are "surrounded by deviant, delinquent, criminal adults in abusive, violence-ridden, fatherless, Godless, and jobless settings." In turn, DiIulio maintained, they live only for the present moment and put their desires, their pleasure, above all else, placing "zero value on the lives of their victims, whom they reflexively dehumanize as just so much worthless [trash]."

Other observers have similarly described the phenomenon of "children without a conscience." These descriptions resonate with much of the public; they seem to be borne out in every additional news story about a senseless act of violence perpetrated by a young criminal who shows no remorse. And statistics seem to confirm the contention that juveniles are growing increasingly violent. Between 1984 and 1994, for example, juvenile homicides tripled.

Although everyone concedes that the worst offenders—the "super-predators" or "children without

DRUGS AND JUVENILE CRIME

Although much of the public believes that illegal drugs are a direct cause of juvenile crime, research doesn't support that view. "Drug use does not cause the initiation of delinquent behavior, nor delinquent behavior the initiation of drug use," according to the Office of Juvenile Justice and Delinquency Prevention. In reality, experts say, minor delinquency usually precedes the beginning of drug use.

However, there is a correlation between drug use and juvenile crime. In a 1987 survey of children in custody in state-operated institutions, for example, 48 percent admitted being under the influence of drugs or alcohol when they committed the offense for which they were institutionalized. Drug use, experts say, prolongs delinquent behavior once it has begun. Drugs alter perception and can lower inhibitions, and youths who already have a high need for stimulation and risk-taking may take additional, criminal risks under the influence of drugs.

In addition, drugs play a more indirect role in the commission of juvenile crime. The illegal-drug trade is a hugely profitable enterprise that employs large numbers of juveniles in its distribution networks. Competition for market share is fierce, and disputes are typically resolved through violent means. The drug trade has thus contributed to the rise in juvenile crime and violence, experts believe.

a conscience"—are a small minority, some observers warn of a looming juvenile "crime bomb" that will explode in the first decade of the next century if current trends continue. This prediction is based on research indicating that 6 percent of the boys born in any given year will be responsible for half the serious crimes and two-thirds of the violent crimes committed by the entire group through age 18. Between the ages of 14 and 17, boys are particularly prone to crime. Because the number of boys in that age group will rise by half a million in the year 2000, we can expect a large increase in serious juvenile crime. Specifically, that year will see "30,000 more muggers, killers, and thieves," predicted James Q. Wilson of the University of California at Los Angeles in a 1994 article in the journal *Commentary*.

But, according to John DiIulio, the predicted increase in the number of serious juvenile criminals is only part of the reason for concern. Because each successive generation of crime-prone boys has experienced greater "moral poverty" than the last, the level of violence they commit is also greater—specifically, DiIulio maintains, about three times greater. So we can expect juvenile crime to increase not only because of simple demographics but also because of the emergence of a generation of lethal super-predators.

Not everyone agrees with this assessment. Some experts dismiss these fears of a generation of predatory youths as greatly exaggerated, if not totally unfounded. A very small percentage of kids, they point out, are involved in violent crimes. In 1994, for example, less than 0.5 percent of all juveniles in the United States were arrested for violent offenses. And, while the 1995 Bureau of the Census estimated that 26 percent of the nation's population was under 18, juveniles accounted for just 14 percent of the violent crime clearances that year, according to the FBI's Uniform Crime Report. (A crime is considered cleared when a suspect is

This bullet-riddled Los Angeles street sign bears mute witness to a shootout between rival youth gangs that claimed the life of a three-year-old bystander. According to some authorities, soaring juvenile homicide rates are largely attributable to a single factor: the ready availability of guns.

arrested and ordered to appear in court or before other authorities.) In other words, adults are responsible for more violent crime, both numerically (as would be expected because they make up more of the population) and proportionally.

As journalists John Hubner and Jill Wolfson point out in their 1996 book *Somebody Else's Children*, "Each generation tends to think that the younger generation is the worst ever." This is an impression that the media tend to reinforce:

> Looking back over a hundred years of headlines in major newspapers, one comes upon "juvenile crime waves" at regular intervals. A century ago, newspapers were railing about street urchins who were as dangerous as wolf packs. In 1924, the Leopold-Loeb murder case in Chicago sparked outrage across the country as hand-wringing editorial writers held up the two teenage "thrill" killers as symbols of an entire generation that was spoiled, lost, and depraved.

Although this view of a younger generation out of control has been a constant throughout the century, "in our current era, the dismay over youth has taken on unprecedented pessimism and outrage," Hubner and Wolfson note. This is attributable in no small measure, the authors claim, to ever-increasing print- and broadcast-media coverage of juvenile crimes—particularly the most senseless and sensational ones—which gives the impression that kids in general are becoming more and more dangerous. As evidence of this phenomenon, Hubner and Wolfson cite a 1994 study published by Children Now, a nonpartisan policy and advocacy group. The study, which tracked coverage of children in five major newspapers and on three television networks over the course of one month, found that 48 percent of the TV stories and 40 percent of the newspaper stories "equated children with crime and violence."

Such overcoverage, critics charge, makes the recent rise in violent juvenile crime appear more severe than it really is. Indeed, not everyone is convinced that there has been a recent rise in violent juvenile crime at all. In *Images and Reality: Juvenile Crime, Youth Violence, and Public Policy*, Michael A. Jones and Barry Krisberg of the National Council on Crime and Delinquency make precisely this case. Instead of gauging crime trends through arrest statistics from the FBI's Uniform Crime Reports—as do many who talk about a "youth crime bomb"—Jones and Krisberg believe that the Justice Department's National Crime Victimization Survey provides a more accurate picture. And data from that survey indicate that violent crime in 1992 was about the same as it had been in 1982.

According to Jones and Krisberg, the FBI's arrest statistics overstate the level of violent juvenile crime in part because they "represent the *number of juveniles* arrested for violent crime—not the *number of violent crimes* committed by young people." When three kids are arrested for killing a store owner during a robbery, for example, that shows up as three homicide arrests, not one homicide. And teenagers commit violent crimes in groups much more often than do older offenders.

All sides in the youth crime debate concede that the total number of homicides committed by juveniles has risen sharply in the last decade. For some experts this is strong evidence that America's youth are indeed growing more brutal, that theories about increasing numbers of super-predators and children without consciences are correct.

Other experts disagree. They maintain that, beyond demographic factors, the increase in juvenile homicides is attributable almost exclusively to the proliferation of guns in the hands of kids, a phenomenon that presumably began in the mid-1980s with the wide-scale recruitment of young street dealers by crack cocaine gangs. Between 1984 and 1994, juvenile murders committed with guns tripled. During the same period, juvenile murders that didn't involve guns remained about the same—and, in fact, those rates have remained steady since the mid-1970s.

Today, more than 80 percent of juvenile killers use a gun, and in various studies a majority of juvenile offenders incarcerated for all types of crime admitted to having carried a gun. Equally sobering are studies indicating that as many as one in five inner-city schoolchildren have access to a gun. According to commentators Hubner and Wolfson,

> America's problem is not teenagers who are wild in the streets, teenagers who can't be rehabilitated, teenagers who are lost causes. What's changed . . . is that kids today can settle their disputes and personal problems in a permanent way, with guns.

CHILDREN AND CRIME: TWO CASE STUDIES

If guns have played an important role in increasing the number of juvenile homicides, gangs have been identified as another cause of rising juvenile violence. For example, teenage-gang-related killings have almost quadrupled since 1980, and of 20,043 homicides listed in the FBI's Uniform Crime Report for 1995, a total of 1,157—more than 5 percent—are described as juvenile gang killings. That number is up from 840 in 1991.

Most discussions of juvenile gangs—and of juvenile criminals in general—center on boys. Although statistically there is a valid explanation for this (only about one in seven juveniles arrested is a girl, for example), female gang membership nationwide may be as high as 15,000, and violent crime rates are rising faster among girls than among boys.

Leticia, a Latina girl living in a small city in Southern California, exemplifies both trends. At the age of 12 she began her criminal career, as well as her

Female gang members congregate on a stoop in The Bronx, New York. Violent crime is rising faster among girls than among boys, and gang membership contributes to the problem.

27

entanglement with a gang, on a dare. On that occasion she and her best friend, Julieta, also 12, were challenged by some older, gang-affiliated girls to do a "rush," a fast, risky crime. That still summer night, as her mother lay sound asleep, Leticia stole down the stairs and stepped out into the cool, empty street. Julieta stood waiting at the corner as planned. It was 3:00 A.M.

In whispers, the girls repeated the plan. They were going to rob an elderly neighbor. They'd enter her house through a downstairs window that Leticia knew she kept unlocked, even during the night. Because the neighbor, Miss Betty, knew Leticia but not Julieta, they agreed that Julieta would do whatever talking might be necessary. If they had to subdue Miss Betty, Leticia would use the hammer her friend had brought along. To conceal their faces the girls would slip panty hose over their heads.

Getting into Miss Betty's house proved easy. The real trouble began in the old woman's bedroom, when Julieta made a little too much noise while rummaging through the bureau for valuables. Miss Betty awoke and, realizing that someone was in her room, began to scream for help.

After hesitating for just a moment, Leticia raised the hammer and brought it down hard on Miss Betty's shoulder. The old woman cried out in pain. When Miss Betty began to plead and scream, Leticia hit her again and again. She took care not to hit near Miss Betty's head; instead, she whacked ferociously at the old woman's upraised arms and legs until the screams were reduced to moans and then to silence.

Meanwhile, Julieta had found a gold necklace, $50, and a credit card. She raised them high above her head like trophies.

The two girls whooped with excitement as they bounded down the stairs and exited proudly through the front door. A short time later, they joined the gang-bangers who had challenged them to do the rush

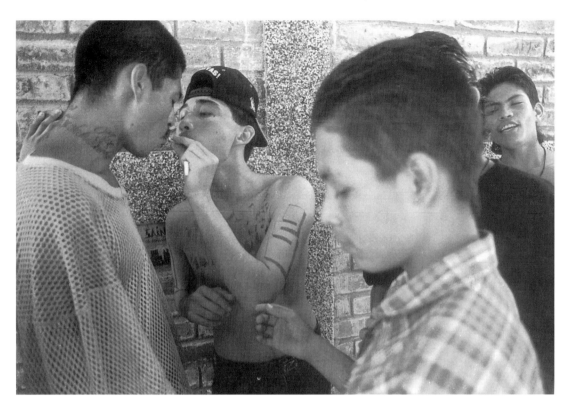

and smoked a few celebratory joints. Looking back on the incident two years afterward, Leticia confessed to a probation officer that though she knew she had hurt Miss Betty, she had felt only elation at accomplishing her first rush. As it turned out, Miss Betty wasn't permanently injured in the attack, and—probably out of fear of retaliation—she never reported the crime.

A few months after that first rush, two gang girls asked Leticia, now 13, to accompany them to another neighborhood. They'd be looking for a certain girl who had scuffled with a member of their gang. It would be dangerous, they cautioned, but this only excited Leticia, who readily agreed. That afternoon they found the girl they were looking for walking by herself. When Leticia's two companions jumped the girl and began hitting and kicking her, Leticia joined in, and by the time they were through, the girl's face was bruised and

Hanging out and using drugs are two time-honored gang activities, as these Salvadoran gang-bangers demonstrate. When rival gangs and readily available guns are added to the mix, the results can be deadly.

bleeding. After that incident, Leticia was considered a part of the gang, a group of six other Latina girls ranging in age from 13 to 17, who hung around together, drank and got high, fought with other groups of girls, and occasionally committed small crimes for money.

The motivations kids have for joining a gang vary, but risk factors identified by experts include poverty, school failure, domestic violence, low self-esteem, and the absence of adult involvement—some of the same factors implicated in juvenile crime in general. Leticia was looking for excitement, esteem, and a sense of belonging, none of which she could find at home. Her mother, left permanently disabled when Leticia's father attacked her with a baseball bat on Leticia's sixth birthday, had limited energy to devote to her two children under the best of circumstances. But when

Although violent crimes draw far more media attention, juveniles commit crimes against property—such as burglary and vandalism—in far greater numbers.

Leticia's 16-year-old sister, Veronica, got pregnant, that crisis overwhelmed her mother, and Leticia was left totally unsupervised. Leticia hadn't seen her father in more than five years, since he'd been accused of sexually molesting Veronica. In her gang Leticia found a surrogate family that, she felt, cared about her.

Accurate statistics on gangs are difficult to come by, but a recent estimate placed gang membership at about 250,000 nationwide. Historically, juvenile gangs were largely an inner-city problem, but recently they have emerged in all areas of the country. Many kids who join gangs have dismal or nonexistent economic opportunities or feel physically vulnerable in their neighborhoods, two other reasons cited for gang membership. Although membership in a gang may entail risking injury or death, many gang members are unconcerned with these dangers, since they don't see themselves as having a future anyway.

Just as children join gangs for different reasons, the structures and activities of gangs vary greatly. Although Leticia's gang wasn't as criminally oriented as many others, it still got her into trouble. She stopped going to school and began spending nearly all her time with her gang friends. A long-running turf dispute with a rival gang of girls erupted in periodic clashes. During one of these fights, Leticia was cut under the eye with a broken bottle. The incident scared her enough that afterward she stayed at home for several days. Soon, however, she was again running the streets with her gang.

One night an off-duty cop stumbled upon Leticia and another girl trying to steal a car stereo. When he identified himself and ordered the two girls to halt, they took off. Leticia's partner got away, but the cop managed to run down Leticia.

At the police station, Leticia initially denied that she had done anything wrong. She claimed that the car's headlights had been on, and when the policeman arrived she was merely turning them off so the battery wouldn't die. She had run because she was afraid he would accuse her of breaking the car's window—in reality, she maintained, it had already been broken. And she denied that another girl had been with her.

It was a ridiculous story, especially since the police recovered a screwdriver in the car and the stereo had been pried from the dashboard. Eventually Leticia confessed, although she steadfastly refused to acknowledge that she had an accomplice.

When a juvenile is picked up for a minor offense such as vandalism or drunkenness, authorities have considerable latitude in handling the situation. They may, for example, opt not to book the child but instead arrange for an informal settlement. This is what the officer handling Leticia's case decided to do. He spoke with the owner of the car, who agreed not to press charges if Leticia would pay for the damage she had done; then he talked to Leticia's mother, who agreed to the restitution and assured him that her daughter had never done anything like this before and wouldn't in the future. Before releasing her into her mother's custody, the policeman warned the 13-year-old to stay out of trouble. Leticia had spent a night in a holding cell at the police station. This, the policeman hoped, would scare her out of repeating her behavior.

It didn't. Only two weeks later, Leticia and the six other members of her gang assaulted two brothers, ages 12 and 13, on a playground after the boys called one of the gang girls a *puta*. Both boys were severely beaten during the attack, and the 12-year-old was unconscious when the paramedics arrived. This time Leticia would end up in court.

Although violent crimes such as the gang assault Leticia participated in and the murder Terrance committed attract the most attention, juveniles commit property crimes in much higher numbers. Of the 677,226 juvenile arrests in 1995 for index crimes,

561,634, or 83 percent, were for property crimes—burglary, larceny-theft, motor vehicle theft, and arson. Of these, arson is perhaps the most troubling. According to the 1995 Unified Crime Report, juveniles were responsible for an astounding 47 percent of the arson cases cleared nationwide. By comparison, only 9 percent of the murders cleared were committed by juveniles.

Jason, a white kid living in the suburbs of an eastern city with his mother, stepfather, and two younger half-brothers, was 14 when he started a major arson fire. Signs of trouble had been present for some time, however. Beginning at age 10, Jason had been picked up by police on various occasions for status offenses. (Status offenses are activities that are illegal only for juveniles—for example, drinking alcohol, being truant, or violating curfew.) There had been the time he and a friend were caught in a mall parking lot

According to the FBI's Uniform Crime Report for 1995, juveniles accounted for about half of the arson arrests nationwide. Arson can indicate a high level of emotional disturbance.

drinking a bottle of wine; the time he skipped school for nearly six weeks; the time he ran away from home, making it as far as a city bus terminal before being picked up.

In addition to these status offenses, Jason had been involved in setting a fire on the playground of the elementary school he had attended, shortly after his 13th birthday. At dusk on a Saturday, he and some friends had wrapped toilet paper around the wooden playground equipment—the bars, the seesaw, and even the tiny castle for the little kids—doused it with gasoline, and set it on fire.

Someone near the school had quickly called the fire department, but the equipment was destroyed before the blaze could be extinguished. Although the boys had dispersed at the first sound of sirens, a neighbor had recognized one of them, and when that child was picked up by the police, he readily named all the others involved.

Initially Jason had been charged with arson, but that charge was reduced to reckless endangerment because he admitted his role and because damage had been confined to the playground. Jason was placed on probation and ordered to pay restitution.

This didn't stop him from setting additional fires, but he did become more careful. From time to time—always late at night when nobody would be around—he and a friend named Jeff would walk to a nearby shopping center with some matches and a soda bottle full of gasoline. Behind the stores, out of view of the parking lot and the street, was a line of dumpsters. Jason and Jeff would set a dumpster on fire, watch the flames for a couple of minutes, and walk home via the tree-lined field at the back of the shopping center.

None of these fires compared with the one Jason set in the early hours of a summer morning after he turned 14. For several weeks he had lain awake at night thinking about setting a big fire; he admitted later he didn't know why. In the shopping center where he and Jeff set their dumpster fires was a storefront at the far end of the complex; it had been vacant since the previous occupant, a restaurant, had closed about two months before. While his family slept, Jason got out of bed, dressed, and quietly went outside. In the garage he grabbed the two-gallon gas can and a bag of oily rags his stepfather used when working on the car.

At the shopping center, Jason soaked the rags with gas, then hurled the gas can through the plate glass window. He threw all but one of the rags into the store, carefully lit the remaining rag and tossed it in, and ran toward the field behind the shopping center.

The blaze turned out to be quite spectacular, engulfing not only the vacant restaurant but also spreading to the adjacent store. A half hour after he had set the fire, Jason returned to the scene, joining a handful of bystanders at the far end of the parking lot as one, then two, then three fire companies battled the inferno.

What should society do with juvenile offenders like Jason, Leticia, and Terrance? Should they be handled by criminal courts and punished as harshly as adults who commit similar crimes? Or should the emphasis be on rehabilitating them, on salvaging their young lives? Are juvenile criminals themselves victims, and if so, to what extent should a child's troubled background figure in the way he or she is treated by the justice system? The answers to these and other important questions have shifted over time, as America has thought and rethought how best to deal with children and crime.

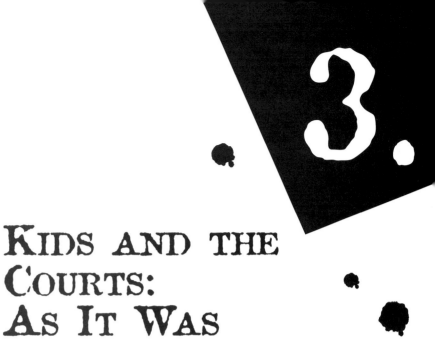

KIDS AND THE COURTS: AS IT WAS

This 1877 woodcut depicts police arresting a juvenile delinquent as his mother pleads for his release. Regardless of his age or offense, the boy would most likely have been prosecuted and incarcerated just like an adult criminal.

Historically, both the legal methods of assigning blame and responsibility to youths who commit crimes and the punishment of these youths have varied considerably in America. During the colonial period and through the early days of the Republic in the late 18th century, children seven years and older were viewed as miniature adults, fully responsible for their behavior. If accused of a crime, they stood trial in criminal court. If found guilty, they might face prison or even death, just like adults. Children under seven were considered "infants," too young to reason and therefore to have criminal intent, so they could not be prosecuted or punished by the legal system.

By today's standards, much of the behavior that could land a child in court and expose him or her to draconian punishment seems fairly innocuous. Among the Puritans of colonial Massachusetts, for example, disrespect for a parent was a capital offense.

Early jails housed criminals of all kinds—violent and nonviolent, male and female, old and young—together. Thus a child as young as seven could be forced into the company of habitual adult offenders, with little or no effort made to ensure that the child was not victimized.

As ideas about children and childhood changed, laws struggled to keep pace. A 19th-century reform movement brought about a big alteration: children were no longer seen as miniature adults but rather as people who were not fully mature, or, in the terms of the Enlightenment philosopher John Locke, as *tabulae rasae*, "blank slates" upon which their experiences were written to form their adult minds. This belief had profound implications for the treatment of juvenile offenders. Placing children side by side with hardened adult criminals no longer seemed to make much sense, for the adults' corrupting influence would likely lead the children, who were still incompletely formed and could therefore be redeemed, into a life of criminality.

By the 1820s, the Society for the Prevention of Juvenile Delinquency had become a strong proponent of separating juvenile and adult criminal offenders. In 1825 another organization, the Society for the Reformation of Juvenile Delinquents, attempted to reform criminal boys by removing them from the New York slums where they lived and having them work in a trade. At night, the boys slept in a large reformatory school. During the day, they went to work in the shops of nearby manufacturers. However well-meaning the society's efforts may have been, the program proved a failure. The manufacturers exploited the children by making them work long hours at grueling and repetitive tasks, and all the boys' wages went to the superintendent of the reformatory. Not surprisingly, many of the boys ran away. Despite this, privately run reformatories sprang up in cities around the country. Soon, however, concern about abuses at these facilities

had forced most of them to close.

As the 1800s unfolded, conditions in many of the nation's cities deteriorated. Large numbers of poor people, including many recent immigrants, crowded into the dilapidated, unsanitary, and disease-ridden slums, struggling to find even the most menial and low-paying jobs in factories and sweatshops. Frequently children, too, toiled long hours in exploitative workplaces. With all the poverty, squalor, and desperation, the slums became breeding grounds for crime. Much of it was committed by kids.

In many cities "street urchins" and gangs of young toughs had, by the late 1800s, made passing through certain neighborhoods a dicey proposition for "respectable" people. Assaults and robberies by juveniles were common, and often police departments were unable or unwilling to maintain order in the worst neighborhoods.

Increasingly, reformers began connecting the

Three homeless children sleep in New York's tenement district in this photograph from the 1890s. Nineteenth-century reformers increasingly connected the problem of juvenile crime and delinquency with the horrible conditions in the nation's slums. Instead of punishing wayward children, they reasoned, why not simply remove them from the environment that had caused their antisocial behavior?

Reform school, 1961. In theory, the juvenile justice system acted in the best interests of each child. As the system evolved, however, social workers and judges came to have nearly unlimited discretion—in juvenile court, children had no rights, no proof was required to establish their guilt, and they couldn't appeal. The four children in this photo may have done nothing more serious than skipping school, for which they could be incarcerated until age 21.

problem of children and crime with the horrendous conditions in the nation's slums. Instead of punishing young criminals, they reasoned, why not rescue the children from the environment that had caused their criminal behavior in the first place?

In 1899 Cook County, Illinois, which includes the city of Chicago, set up the first juvenile court in the United States under the doctrine of the state as parent (*parens patriae*). By tradition, a child's parents had always been viewed not only as having the right to treat the child as they saw fit, but also as being best equipped to look after the child's welfare, and the law had been reluctant to interfere in family matters. But with the application of *parens patriae*, the state was asserting that in certain cases the parents weren't the best judges of what was good for the child, and in those cases the state would step in. For the first time, delinquent children would be treated differently from adult criminals; now the state would consider their welfare. Punishment would be replaced by rehabilitation; the children would be saved from the pernicious influence of their environment.

The idea spread throughout the country. By 1925 all but two states had initiated probation programs, juvenile courts, or both. The juvenile courts had—and continue to have—a dual mandate: to make custody decisions in cases of parental abuse and neglect, and to deal with juvenile delinquency. As early as the 1920s, however, juvenile courts could waive jurisdiction to adult court when a child was accused of an extremely serious offense.

As juvenile courts evolved, the procedures they followed diverged more and more from those followed in the nation's adult courts. Trials conducted in adult courts were adversarial proceedings, with lawyers for the defense and prosecution arguing before a jury that the evidence supported a finding of innocence or guilt. Rules of evidence and procedural safeguards protected the defendants' rights. In juvenile court, on the other hand, everyone was—at least in theory—interested in the same outcome: doing what was best for the child. So there was no need for safeguards to protect the children's rights (in fact, the children had no rights), no need for lawyers to argue about the evidence, no need for a jury to decide innocence or guilt. In fact, in juvenile court children weren't deemed guilty at all. Rather, they were considered delinquent—not in accord with the law—a subtle distinction perhaps, but nonetheless one that emphasized the juvenile court's special mandate.

Unlike adult trials, juvenile court hearings were confidential, in order to protect the child from being stigmatized. Typically, no transcript of the proceedings was made, all records were sealed, and the hearings were closed to the public and press.

Before a juvenile hearing, a social worker would generally investigate the child's home and school life, and based on these and other social factors, as well as the child's offense, the judge would decide what the juvenile's treatment needs were. In juvenile court there were no mandated or fixed sentences, and children deemed delinquent weren't sent to prison with adults. Rather, they were sent to reformatories or training schools until they were "cured" or turned 21.

Gradually, pre-delinquent behavior fell under court jurisdiction. Such behavior included truancy and "the possibility of leading an immoral life," neither of which constituted a crime for adults. Because the children had no legal rights, the system could be cruelly arbitrary. For example, a social worker investigating a boy who had skipped school might decide that the boy's home life was less than ideal, and based on this opinion a juvenile court judge might take the child away from his family and send him to a training school. Because social workers and judges came predominantly from the middle classes and juvenile delinquents from the urban poor, decisions could be based on little more than cultural differences—a social worker's or judge's bias that a "normal" family was one that had middle-class values and lived a middle-class lifestyle.

Such potential abuses notwithstanding, juvenile courts operated under the doctrine of *parens patriae* into the 1960s. The case that would radically change the juvenile justice system began innocently enough, with a childish prank. One afternoon in rural Gila County, Arizona, 15-year-old Gerald Gault and a friend decided to make a crank phone call. They called their neighbor, a married woman, and asked her, "Are your cherries ripe today? Do you have big bombers?"

After the woman lodged a complaint, the Gila County sheriff arrested Gerald Gault, charging him as a juvenile delinquent and placing him in detention.

At the hearing a week later, neither the woman nor Gerald's friend testified, although Gerald's parents had requested that the neighbor appear so that their son could counter her testimony. In fact, it was never established that Gerald Gault had made the suggestive phone call. Nevertheless, the judge proclaimed him "habitually immoral," because of this charge and another two years before—never proven—that Gerald had stolen another boy's baseball bat and glove.

Two children charged with being among a gang of 17 youths who savagely beat a pair of groundskeepers in a New York park are led into a police station. By law, the identities of juvenile offenders, even those accused of high-profile crimes, are kept secret in most cases. This confidentiality, a hallmark of the juvenile justice system since the first years of the 20th century, has come under increasing criticism.

Gerald Gault was sentenced to a state training school, the equivalent of a juvenile prison, for six years until he came of age. Had he been an adult when he made the call, he would have received a maximum sentence of a $50 fine or two months in jail.

Gerald had been presumed guilty. He would not have been permitted an attorney for the hearing had he requested one, and no transcript of the proceedings was made. He had no right to confront his accuser in court and no right to an appeal. This was standard operating procedure for juvenile courts, the judge told the stunned family.

Not content to accept the ruling, Gerald's parents filed a suit asserting that the proceedings had violated their son's constitutional rights. The Arizona Supreme Court rejected the suit, but the case made it to the U.S. Supreme Court three years after the crank call was made. In 1967, in a landmark decision, the Court ruled that juveniles could not be convicted without due process—without a fair trial, without evidence of their guilt, without a lawyer, without a chance to question witnesses, and without the right to protect themselves from self-incrimination. "Under our Constitution, the condition of being a boy does not justify a kangaroo court," read the decision, which also rejected the doctrine of *parens patriae* as being unclear.

The Supreme Court's *In re Gault* decision transformed juvenile justice. While the notion that juvenile courts should do what was in the child's best interests persisted, the very fact that delinquent children were accorded most of the legal rights of adult defendants made juvenile court much more adversarial, like adult court. The presence of defense attorneys led to the inclusion of prosecutors, and for the first time the state actually had to establish that the juvenile had committed the offense in question. Juvenile hearings had become, for all intents and purposes, trials.

Three years after *In re Gault,* the *Winship* decision further closed the gap between adult and juvenile justice by extending another crucial adult right to minors—that "proof beyond a reasonable doubt" be necessary for conviction.

While changes to the juvenile justice system were occurring as the result of Supreme Court mandates, politicians were seeking effective legislative and governmental responses to juvenile crime. In 1948 President Harry Truman convened the Mid-Century Conference on Children and Youth. Among the issues it considered were developing appropriate police services for juveniles and involving social services in crime prevention. The conference urged the federal government to take a stronger role, but Congress didn't act on this recommendation.

Finally, more than a decade later, Congress passed the Juvenile Delinquency and Youth Offenses Control Act in 1961. It offered funds for demonstration projects to be created by state and local governments as well as by private agencies.

Concern about juvenile crime ebbed in the 1960s,

when the nation's attention focused largely on the civil rights movement and the Vietnam War, but by 1974 juvenile crime was again considered a national problem. There had been a huge rise in the arrest rate for violent juveniles—an increase of 216 percent in the 15-year period from 1960 to 1974. In addition, up to 40 percent of incarcerated juveniles had not committed any crime but were being held for status offenses or while awaiting a custody hearing, and there were no limits on how long a juvenile could be held before appearing before a judge. To address these problems, Congress passed the Juvenile Justice and Delinquency Prevention Act of 1974. The act sought to reduce juvenile crime and to address the way juveniles were handled by the judicial system. Specifically, placing juvenile offenders in a variety of community programs and taking them out of detention became a priority. The "least restrictive alternative" was deemed the best.

The act was reauthorized and given a boost in funding in 1977. In 1980 it was revised so that juveniles would be removed from adult jails and lockup facilities.

However, 1981 saw the beginning of a trend to reduce funding for the act, along with a shift in emphasis from delinquency prevention to criminal justice. Reform and rehabilitation were giving way to punishment.

Today, the juvenile justice system is undergoing another shift, one whose goal is to balance the best interests of the child with the best interests of society. Debate over how exactly this can be accomplished is often heated. Each state has its own mandates, so the same crime can lead to vastly different outcomes for juvenile offenders in different places. In general, though, the trend has been for states to enact stricter penalties for juvenile criminals, particularly when their crimes are violent. And more legislatures are clamoring to have serious juvenile offenders removed from juvenile court entirely.

Juvenile Justice Today— Through the Courts

Had he committed his crime 20 years ago, things would likely have turned out quite differently for Terrance, who was charged with murdering his young tormentor Joe with a handgun. Two decades ago, Terrance's case would have been decided by a judge in a juvenile court, and the maximum penalty he could have received would have been imprisonment until he turned 25.

Currently, however, the laws in Terrance's state specify that the cases of 15-year-olds charged with murder automatically go to adult criminal court. Because the district attorney viewed Terrance's crime as premeditated—he had taken Aunt Wanda's gun to school for the express purpose of dealing with Joe in the afternoon—a charge of first-degree murder was filed, as were aggravated assault and weapons charges. Terrance faced the possibility of life imprisonment.

Terrance had previously appeared in juvenile court and had been adjudicated delinquent for a robbery he

A multitude of rules and procedures govern the dispensing of juvenile justice. For lawyers, probation officers, social workers, psychologists, and other insiders, the rules prevent access to any child's complete records. For outsiders they often make the whole system unfathomable.

and a friend had committed. For that crime he had been placed on probation. But because this was his first time in adult court, the murder of Joe was considered his first offense. That, combined with his youth and testimony about Joe's verbal provocations, made Terrance's public defender optimistic that the district attorney would accept a plea bargain. She was right, and Terrance pled guilty to second-degree murder, avoiding a trial; the other charges were dropped. He was sentenced to 17 to 24 years in state prison.

Leticia, arrested for her role in the gang assault on two young boys, had been sent to the youth detention center, where minors are held pending the disposition of their cases. By law a hearing had to be held within three days of Leticia's arrest. At the hearing, the juvenile court judge listened as an assistant district attorney presented a delinquency petition, which outlined the state's reasons for wanting Leticia held for a delinquency hearing. (The process is similar to arraignment in the adult criminal justice system, during which the state presents its charges against a suspect, the suspect may answer them by entering a plea, and a judge decides whether there is sufficient grounds for ordering a trial.) The district attorney stated that Leticia was charged with aggravated assault. Because her family had no money, Leticia was represented by a young public defender, whom she had met right before the hearing began. He said little, and in the end the judge ordered that a delinquency hearing be held. The entire procedure had lasted less than five minutes.

Unlike adults, juveniles have no right to bail. Depending on the offense and the juvenile's family, judges sometimes release minors into the custody of their parents before their delinquency hearing. But because Leticia's mother hadn't appeared at the preliminary hearing, the judge ordered Leticia sent back to the youth detention center.

The youth detention center for the county in

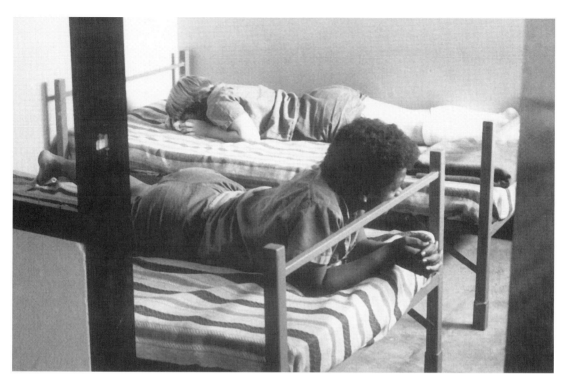

which Leticia lived is a four-story facility located three blocks from the juvenile justice building that houses the juvenile courtrooms. It has 425 beds and usually operates at or near capacity. The boys and girls are housed in separate wings.

Various soft touches like pastel-colored corridors cannot disguise the center's primary function: it is a jail. In the control room, guards monitor the kids' activities through closed-circuit TV screens and lock and unlock doors with electronic switches.

Two units in the boys' wing and one unit in the girls' wing house the violent offenders: murderers, rapists, those who have assaulted staff members. Security in these units is particularly tight.

Although Leticia was accused of aggravated assault, she didn't qualify for the high-security unit. Instead, she shared a cell in a regular unit with a 14-year-old white girl who was there for possession of cocaine.

Girls at Philadelphia's Youth Study Center, a detention facility that houses juveniles while they await their hearings.

As with prisons everywhere, regimentation was a fact of life in the youth detention center, and Leticia confessed that this aspect of her incarceration—even more than the boredom of being away from her friends—was most difficult to adjust to. At the same time each day, she had to get up, she had to shower, she had to march with the other girls to the cafeteria to eat her three daily meals. She had to attend the center's school. She had to wear the uniform—light blue pants, white T-shirt, cheap white canvas sneakers. She had to be in her cell with the lights off at the same time each night. Recreation periods—the only times she could do what she wanted—occupied only a couple hours each day.

During her incarceration at the youth detention center, Leticia met several times with her new court-appointed lawyer, a tall, middle-aged woman with short, graying hair. The lawyer asked Leticia numerous questions about her crime and her gang activities. She seemed particularly interested in how and why Leticia had joined the gang and whether the older girls had pressured her into doing illegal things. With her lawyer Leticia was brusque, sarcastic, and at times downright rude, as though she really didn't care what happened to her, but as a juvenile justice professional the lawyer had seen countless troubled kids act this way before.

Six months after her arrest, Leticia, handcuffed, was driven the three blocks from the youth detention center to the juvenile justice building along with nine other girls whose cases were also scheduled to be heard that day. Leticia's day in court had finally arrived.

The waiting wasn't quite over yet, however. Leticia and the other girls were placed in a holding cell, where they would remain until a judge was ready to hear their individual cases. Leticia sat at the end of one of the wooden benches, rested her head in her hands, and stared at the floor. Several of the older girls—the ones who had been through the juvenile courts before—

After a juvenile is adjudicated delinquent, a probation officer investigates the offender's home situation, assessing the stresses and supports in the child's life. At the dispositional hearing, the judge considers the findings of the probation officer and other specialists in determining how best to treat the child.

talked and laughed loudly, but Leticia was in no mood for conversation. For the first time, she was genuinely nervous about what would happen to her.

Periodically, a bailiff would appear outside the holding cell, call out a name, and lead that girl away. Eventually Leticia's name was called.

Leticia followed the bailiff down a corridor, up two flights of stairs, and into the courtroom where her case would be heard. A small, bright room with a row of windows on the left, it didn't project the solemn weight of a criminal court. Two small tables, one for Leticia and her lawyer and one for the assistant district attorney who would be functioning as a prosecutor, stood in front of the judge's elevated desk, alongside of which was the witness box. A few seats at the back of the room were for family and witnesses; in one of them sat Leticia's mother. No one not directly involved in the case attended the hearing. There was no jury box, as juveniles, unlike adults, don't have the right to a trial by jury; the judge alone would decide the case.

The judge, an intense but kind-looking man who appeared to be in his mid-fifties, said good morning to Leticia, her lawyer, and the assistant district attorney. He then explained that today's hearing would focus only on the facts: what had happened on the playground when the two boys were assaulted, and was Leticia involved? If the evidence presented in court supported the charge that Leticia had committed aggravated assault, she would be adjudicated delinquent, and then another proceeding, called a dispositional hearing, would be held to determine what treatment she would receive. If the evidence presented today was insufficient, Leticia would be released.

The assistant district attorney called as witnesses the two brothers, who detailed the events on the playground that led to the assault by the gang of girls. Both boys testified that they had gone to school with Leticia, so they recognized her as one of their attackers. The older boy claimed that after his brother had fallen to the ground, the girls kicked him in the head and ribs until he was no longer moving. Then, the older boy testified, he saw Leticia pick up his brother's head by the hair and slam it down onto the pavement. During this testimony, the judge, unlike typical judges in criminal court, took an active role, questioning the witness himself in order to clarify certain points.

In her cross-examination, Leticia's lawyer didn't attempt to refute the contention that her client had been present during the attack, but she asked how, in the midst of a gang assault, the boys could be sure exactly what Leticia had done. She especially found it incredible that the older boy could have seen Leticia smash his brother's head on the ground when he himself was trying to fend off three other girls. For the most part, however, the boys stuck to their original stories.

After the state's witnesses had testified, Leticia's lawyer had the opportunity to call witnesses of her own, but she declined. The only eyewitnesses who might refute the boys' testimony were Leticia and the other gang girls, and she didn't think any of them would make good witnesses. Leticia, she believed, would strike her characteristic pose as a tough kid who didn't care, which wouldn't win any points with the judge. And, if she called the other gang girls, they might mention details that would reinforce Leticia's image as a dangerous gang-banger. The safest thing to do, the lawyer concluded, was to hope the judge would decide that Leticia's involvement in the assault couldn't be established beyond a reasonable doubt.

However, the judge did conclude that Leticia had committed aggravated assault, and he therefore adjudicated her delinquent. A dispositional hearing was scheduled to determine what should be done with her—or, in the language of a court still operating with the vestiges of *parens patriae*, how best to meet her treatment needs. In the meantime, Leticia was sent back to the youth detention center.

Before the dispositional hearing, Leticia met with a probation officer, who asked her about her gang involvement, school, and family life. The probation officer also visited Leticia's house and interviewed her mother and her sister, Veronica, who was now caring for her baby boy. In addition, she visited Leticia's school and talked to her former teachers. Before the dispositional hearing, the probation officer would submit a report about the stresses in Leticia's life, how

Drugs, violence, and a climate of fear plague many of our nation's schools, making learning difficult. School failure, in turn, contributes to juvenile delinquency and crime. Breaking this cycle defies easy solutions.

A probation officer meets with a client. Juvenile courts rely on probation departments to monitor first-time offenders and children whose offenses are relatively minor, as well as kids who have been released from detention. Unfortunately, however, many probation officers carry huge caseloads that make it difficult to give each child the attention he or she might need.

she coped with them, and what support she got from her family. The judge would consider the report's findings in deciding what to do with Leticia.

Leticia also met several times with a court-appointed psychologist, who asked her about how she was adjusting to life in the detention center, what her life had been like before she was arrested, and what she intended to do in the future. The psychologist's report would provide the court with additional insights into Leticia's behavior and needs.

During the dispositional hearing, the probation

officer didn't testify, but the judge summarized her findings: Leticia's family life was relatively stable, if unnurturing and unsupportive. She lived with her mother, older sister, and infant nephew; her father, who had been abusive, had not been with the family for more than seven years. Leticia's mother, who remained impaired from a domestic assault, couldn't adequately supervise her younger daughter; Leticia was permitted to come and go as she pleased. Despite obvious indications to the contrary, her mother continued to deny Leticia's gang involvement. Leticia was chronically truant.

Leticia, for her part, had problems with authority, the probation officer had observed. For example, a former teacher reported that she had once asked Leticia to take off her hat in the classroom and Leticia had refused, marching out of the class and never returning. In explaining why she had done that, Leticia told the probation officer that she didn't have to put up with anyone bossing her around because she didn't have anything to lose—she fully expected to die before the age of 20. When pressed to elaborate, she said she'd probably be killed in a gang fight or would be "snatched"—kidnapped, raped, and murdered.

The psychologist who examined Leticia testified at the dispositional hearing. In her view, Leticia, though she tried to project an image of toughness and nonchalance, suffered from low self-esteem. And, the psychologist maintained, she had the symptoms of post-traumatic stress disorder, an emotional disturbance in which the person relives a traumatic past event or set of events. In Leticia's case, that set of events was the abuse inflicted on her family by her father, particularly the time he smashed her mother's face with a baseball bat, an attack Leticia had witnessed on her sixth birthday. The psychologist also stated that Leticia may have been sexually abused by her father, although she couldn't be sure.

After reading the probation officer's report and hearing the psychologist's testimony, the judge had to decide what would be the best treatment for Leticia—and how society could best be protected from any further criminal behavior on her part. The options ranged from probation to placement in a group home to incarceration in one of the state's juvenile correctional institutions until Leticia came of age.

Two factors in particular concerned the judge. First, there was Leticia's young age, which he viewed as both a reason to do everything possible to help her and a cause for apprehension. The judge was keenly aware of studies indicating that the younger a child is when first arrested—especially for a violent offense—the more likely that child is to become a habitual, dangerous adult criminal. Second, there was Leticia's chronic truancy. As Falcon Baker asserts in the book *Saving Our Kids from Delinquency, Drugs, and Despair*, "School performance is by far the most significant single predictor of delinquency and future criminality—more accurate than race or economic level or social class, more accurate than any of the sociological variables commonly considered to have an effect on the rate of delinquency." This may be true in part because it has to do with behavior, over which kids have some control, unlike nonbehavioral facts of life such as race and class. Yet, as important as academic success is, many of the nation's schools don't provide an ideal climate for learning. For example, more than half of all juvenile victimizations—including one-quarter of the violent victimizations—occur in schools or on school property, according to the Bureau of Justice Statistics. And, in a nationally representative sample, 15 percent of students age 12 to 19 reported that gangs existed in their schools.

His concerns notwithstanding, the judge in Leticia's case opted for probation with strict terms and a stipulation that failure to live up to the terms would result in incarceration. Leticia agreed to attend an alternative school that combined rigid discipline with emotional support. She and her mother agreed to attend therapy sessions to help them work through their unaddressed family issues. In addition, Leticia would be compelled to attend special, supervised programs during her school vacations, the first of which would be a version of Outward Bound, a wilderness program designed to build self-esteem, trust, and an ability to work with others. And Leticia had to maintain regular contact with her probation officer, who would give her rules of conduct she had to follow— including what she could and could not wear, whom she could associate with, and when she had to be at home—and would closely monitor her compliance.

Jason, the 14-year-old arsonist, was already on probation when he set fire to the vacant restaurant. He'd been meeting with his probation officer once a month, and as far as the probation officer could tell, he was making good progress.

Although the juvenile justice system relies on probation officers to balance two crucial, and at times conflicting, functions—acting as informed advocate for troubled children and protecting society from dangerous kids—many probation departments are grossly understaffed and underfunded. While most probation officers have master's degrees and can provide both family and group therapy, the typical caseload of about 40 cases at a time, each potentially involving reams of paperwork, makes it difficult to devote a great deal of attention to every child. Invariably, some children slip through the cracks.

Jason was one of these children. Had she been able to spend more time with him, the probation officer might have picked up on the anger at the heart of Jason's behavior—and been able to get him some help before he started the big fire. Arson often indicates a high level of emotional disturbance, sometimes because of an early history of physical or sexual abuse.

Although Jason had never suffered such abuse, he was traumatized by his parents' bitter divorce, which occurred when he was eight, and he resented his mother's remarriage a year later. He believed that his stepfather was overly strict and that both his step-father and his mother loved his half-brothers—*their* children—but would just as soon have him go away. Indeed, after Jason was arrested for the shopping mall arson, his mother and stepfather, declaring they could no longer control him, told his probation officer that whatever the outcome of his hearing, they wanted him out of their house. Unfortunately, Jason's father also had remarried, and he and his new wife had little interest in seeing this problem child, much less raising him. Jason felt emotionally abandoned.

While Jason was in the youth detention center awaiting his hearing, his probation officer contacted the Center for Arson Research, a Philadelphia-based group, which recommended a specific residential facility for young offenders with profound psychological needs. At his dispositional hearing, the probation officer argued strenuously for placing Jason at this facility. He would attend a special on-site school with a teacher-to-student ratio of 1:5, she said, which would give him a great chance to succeed academically and build his self-esteem. He would attend daily individual and group therapy sessions to help him understand and work through his feelings. And the facility's family-like setting might provide some emotional security.

The judge decided to give this alternative a try. He directed that Jason be placed in the special facility for a period of time to be determined by the facility's staff and the probation officer. After Jason's release, the child welfare department and the probation officer would recommend an appropriate living arrangement for him. A foster home might be an option, though for obvious reasons finding people willing to take in kids with a history of arson can prove difficult.

Jason's future—like that of Leticia and tens of thousands of other juvenile offenders all across America—is anything but certain. It depends not simply on his ability and willingness to change but on a system of supervising, treating, and punishing child lawbreakers that, in the view of many observers, is sometimes unwieldy, often irrational, and increasingly ineffective.

A Balancing Act

There is broad consensus today that juvenile crime is a serious national problem. What isn't so clear is what to do about it. Not surprisingly, the various solutions offered reflect differing assessments of the causes of the problem.

For some time now, many observers have maintained that a large part of the problem lies with the juvenile justice system itself. When that system evolved, the nature of juvenile crime—and indeed, of American society as a whole—differed vastly from conditions today. Juvenile justice institutions, the critics charge, simply haven't kept pace with changes. Now,

Playing the role of drill sergeant, a corrections officer yells at a young offender in a prison-based boot camp in Illinois. As an alternative to traditional prison for certain juvenile criminals, states have experimented with programs that seek to replicate the atmosphere of the military's basic training, during which a recruit's self-identity—including values that are considered undesirable—is systematically broken down and re-formed.

they say, the system merely staggers on, overwhelmed by the sheer volume of cases it handles, laboring under antiquated procedures and rules that serve neither juvenile lawbreakers nor the larger society.

One frequently cited example of how outmoded the juvenile justice system has become is the system's confidentiality rules. Critics believe that these rules, whose original intent was to protect delinquent children from being stigmatized, no longer make sense in a society awash in juvenile violence. Is it logical, for example, that a schoolteacher not know when a student entering her classroom has a history of sexual assault? Or that a kid who commits murder will get a new start—without a criminal record—at age 18? Responding to criticisms such as these, some states have relaxed the rules under which certain individuals or agencies may access juvenile records; some states even release juvenile criminals' names to the media under limited conditions.

Another criticism of the juvenile justice system is that it doesn't adequately discourage crime. It is generally acknowledged that for punishment to be effective, especially with children, it must be quick, consistent, and certain; kids who commit crimes must know that they will be held accountable for their actions. And yet, according to the 1996 Juvenile Justice Action Plan issued by the Coordinating Council on Juvenile Justice and Delinquency Prevention, "the juvenile justice system is often so overwhelmed that juvenile offenders receive no meaningful interventions or consequences, even for relatively serious offenses." And, the plan continues, "[t]his neglect serves neither rehabilitation nor accountability goals."

Today, however, concerns about unmet "rehabilitation goals" quite often take a backseat as critics of the juvenile justice system focus on the need to protect society from violent, predatory juveniles. The only way to accomplish this, they argue, is through appropriately severe punishment. However, even when offenders are

In recent years, politicians and private citizens alike have clamored for harsher penalties for juvenile offenders. This has translated into legislation mandating that increased numbers of juveniles be handled by the adult criminal system. Whether this trend has led to a reduction in crime—or even to longer sentences for young lawbreakers—is hotly debated.

adjudicated delinquent in the juvenile system, they face limited sanctions: the majority receive formal probation, and the maximum penalty the juvenile courts can impose is incarceration until age 21 or, in some cases, age 25. And so dangerous kids are released back into society to commit more crimes, critics charge.

To address the perceived need to "get tough" on juvenile criminals—which, whatever the policy merits, is also, in an era of widespread public fear of crime, a winning political position—state legislators have moved to change the rules governing juvenile justice. The emphasis has been on removing offenders from the "soft" juvenile justice system and placing them in adult criminal court.

New York led this "get tough" trend when, in 1978, it gave criminal courts "original jurisdiction" over juveniles 13 and older who were accused of murder and over juveniles 14 and older who were accused of rape or assault with a deadly weapon. In other words, these kids' cases would automatically go to criminal court. Other states relaxed the conditions under which juveniles could be waived to criminal court by judges after consideration of a motion filed by the prosecutor. Still other states gave prosecutors limited discretionary powers to file cases involving juveniles directly in criminal court.

In addition to the greater punishment it was assumed kids would receive in adult court, which would effectively remove offenders from society for longer periods, these procedures, it was hoped, would reduce crime in two ways: first, kids who had not yet committed serious crimes but might be tempted to do

CHILDREN AND CAPITAL PUNISHMENT

Only three nations currently permit executions for crimes committed by juveniles: Iran, Iraq, and the United States. In 1982 the U.S. Supreme Court decision in *Eddings v. Oklahoma* stated that the "defendant's youthful age should be considered a mitigating factor in deciding whether to apply the death penalty." In other words, juvenile offenders should be treated less severely than adults in capital cases. Two more Supreme Court cases in 1988 and 1989 set 16 as the minimum age for the death penalty.

On May 18, 1990, Dalton Prejean, who had been convicted of murdering a state trooper when he was 17 and killing a taxi driver when he was 14, became the first minor to die, in the electric chair, under the 1989 Supreme Court ruling. As of June 30, 1996, a total of 47 death-row inmates were awaiting execution for crimes they had committed as juveniles.

so would be deterred, realizing that if caught they would face tough adult justice, including the possibility of life in prison or even the death penalty; and second, violent offenders would be less likely to repeat their crimes, having been taught a tough lesson they'd remember if and when they were ultimately released.

Since 1978 at least 41 states have enacted legislation expanding the use of one or more of the mechanisms for putting "serious, violent, and chronic" juvenile offenders in criminal court, and the number of children tried as adults has grown steeply. Increasingly, use of the criminal courts has become a key strategy in the nation's response to juvenile crime. But is it working? The reviews are decidedly mixed.

Critics maintain that even the strategy's most basic assumption—that transferred juveniles would receive harsher punishment in adult court—hasn't been borne out. Adult courts and correctional facilities are themselves overburdened, so minors often benefit from plea bargains designed to avoid the cost of a trial, or they receive probation when a juvenile court might have ordered incarceration. Additionally, critics say, when the offender is young, juries are frequently reluctant to convict.

Some studies comparing the treatment of kids in juvenile and adult courts do indeed document a tendency of adult courts to treat the kids *less* severely. But, as proponents of transferring juvenile offenders correctly point out, these studies are based principally on data from the late 1970s and 1980s, and a few more recent studies do show greater penalties for juveniles tried in adult courts.

Another rationale for trying kids as adults is that the practice produces a deterrent effect: faced with the possibility of incurring more severe sanctions, many children who might be inclined to commit crimes will not. But critics cite a lack of evidence to support this belief. They point out, for example, that Florida and

New York, two states that pioneered treating juvenile criminals as adults and that continue to be among the nation's most punitive toward juvenile offenders, also continue to have the nation's highest rates of violent crime. Many experts assert that among all groups of criminals, juveniles are the least susceptible to deterrence. Yet while no one has adequately demonstrated a deterrent effect, no one has conclusively *disproven* the idea either, and it can be argued that without laws transferring minors to adult court, juvenile crime would be even higher.

Are juveniles who do "adult time" less likely to reoffend than juveniles handled by the juvenile courts, as proponents of transferring juveniles contend? Critics of the policy are skeptical. Once again, they say, there is no evidence to support the contention that rates of recidivism, or reoffending, are lower for juveniles handled in the adult courts. One study, for example, found no difference in rates of rearrest for kids convicted of burglary in adult court and kids adjudicated delinquent for burglary in juvenile court. But kids convicted of robbery in adult court were significantly more likely to be rearrested than their counterparts who had been handled in the juvenile system. Another study on various types of juvenile offenders found higher rates of recidivism as well as increased progression to more serious offenses among those tried as adults than among those handled for similar crimes by the juvenile system. Unfortunately, however, "an inadequate amount of research has been conducted," according to the Coordinating Council on Juvenile Justice and Delinquency Prevention, and the "relative merits of juvenile versus criminal justice system handling of serious, violent, and chronic juvenile offenders are difficult to determine conclusively."

One point that frequently gets lost in discussions of juvenile crime is the fact that what are called "serious, chronic, and violent offenders" constitute a small

minority of the children who come into contact with the justice system. In Los Angeles, for example, an extensive study tracked thousands of first-time juvenile offenders for three years. The researchers found that 57 percent of the kids, once arrested for the first time, were scared enough or smart enough not to encounter the justice system again. In other words, they stayed clean after their first brush with the law. Of the remaining kids, 27 percent got arrested once or twice again, but that was all. They, too, went straight. The final 16 percent went on to become what are termed chronic offenders. Other studies have replicated this finding, with the percentage of chronic offenders ranging up to 23 percent.

Of course, the percentage of chronic offenders in the entire juvenile population is much lower, perhaps 3 to 5 percent, but it is these kids who capture most of the

Three youth offenders lug heavy logs in a drill at the Greene County Impact Incarceration Program in Roodhouse, Illinois. The program and others like it seek to instill self-discipline, self-esteem, and respect for authority through a combination of rigorous exercise, behavior modification, counseling, and job training.

media and public attention and, some observers would argue, drive policy. These are the so-called predators, and society demands protection from them.

Few would argue that incarcerating habitual violent offenders for long periods isn't an appropriate—even a necessary—response, and obviously while a kid is in prison he can't be committing crimes. But, some people argue, in our enthusiasm for getting tough on juvenile criminals, we've cast too wide a net.

Although the argument for trying kids as adults usually centers on the most violent offenders, in reality the percentage of juveniles in criminal court for violent offenses may actually be relatively small. "Nationally, only 38 percent of juveniles whose cases get kicked up to adult courts are charged with committing a violent crime," journalists John Hubner and Jill

RACE AND THE JUVENILE JUSTICE SYSTEM

When many Americans think of juvenile criminals, they think of minority children. While it is true that minorities, particularly African-American and Latino males, are overrepresented in the juvenile justice system, that doesn't necessarily mean that crime rates among these children match their disproportionately high arrest and incarceration rates. According to the Office of Juvenile Justice and Delinquency Prevention, "disproportionate minority confinement tends to result, in part, from a number of discrete decisions made throughout the system, from point of arrest through intake and sentencing."

In other words, the system may be biased, often in subtle ways, against minorities. For instance, a police officer working in a crime-ridden urban neighborhood might be more inclined to arrest a black youth for a minor offense like underage drinking than a police officer working in an affluent suburban neighborhood would be to arrest a white youth engaged in similar behavior. Similarly, an intake officer might be less likely to arrange an informal settlement for a minority kid. And a judge might tend to view minorities as poorer risks than white children and thus to incarcerate them more frequently.

Of course, socioeconomic factors do play a significant role in crime rates, and minorities are disproportionately represented among the nation's poor, particularly its urban poor. And other factors typically seen in economically depressed minority neighborhoods, such as inadequate schools and the prevalence of drugs and guns, contribute to increased juvenile delinquency as well. So the question of minority overrepresentation in the juvenile justice system is much more complex than institutional biases alone.

Wolfson maintain. "The others are crimes against property, like setting fire to a building (41 percent), or drug charges, like selling crack cocaine to an undercover agent (15 percent)."

And the transferral of these nonviolent offenders to the adult system may have severe unintended consequences. Even if they aren't ultimately convicted, these children may be incarcerated with adults while they await the disposition of their cases. And if they are convicted and sentenced to a prison term, they'll do time alongside adult criminals, who may victimize them. According to the Coalition for Juvenile Justice, a governmental committee charged with advising Congress and the president on juvenile justice policy, juveniles "in adult institutions are five times more likely to be sexually assaulted, twice as likely to be beaten by staff, and fifty percent more likely to be attacked with a weapon than youths in a juvenile facility." And counseling services in adult prisons are inadequate for the needs of juveniles. In the end, many experts say, it's not just the kids who suffer. Society, too, eventually pays a price in increased criminality and violence when the kids are released. For, experts maintain, their experiences in prison turn many of these kids into habitual—and, frequently, habitually violent—criminals.

Instead of focusing so heavily on punishment, juvenile justice reformers say, the system should attempt to strike a balance between protecting society from juvenile crime and rehabilitating young offenders. Such a balance might ultimately require limited use of the adult courts, as a truly last resort, but in the main, reformers say, the best hope lies with innovations in the juvenile justice system.

Particularly with younger juvenile offenders, reformers assert, incarceration rarely makes sense as a first option. Not only is locking kids up expensive— incarceration for a year can cost up to $64,000, considerably more than a year's tuition at any of the nation's top colleges—but it also doesn't seem to turn kids away from criminal behavior. In California, for example, 50 percent of previously incarcerated juveniles return to jail; in New York, the rate of recidivism soars as high as 75 percent. This is due in part to the fact that after they are released, the kids are likely to return to the same overwhelming problems they were experiencing before. Therefore, juvenile justice reformers say, a better option is to find ways to help incipient offenders deal with their problems, and in the process head off further criminal behavior.

To date, various innovative programs have been set up to accomplish this goal, and each year more are developed. The programs give probation departments options for getting each offender the kind of help he or she could use most. Examples include school-based boot camps, which are designed to teach self-discipline and build self-esteem and typically involve rigorous exercise, counseling, and G.E.D. training; and the High Impact Program, designed for kids who have used or sold drugs, which emphasizes teamwork as well as life and job skills and which includes a challenging weekend at a wilderness camp, where rock climbing, low and high rope courses, and the like build a sense of personal and community accomplishment.

Many chronic offenders, particularly those who have committed violent crimes, wouldn't be good candidates for programs such as the ones described above. But instead of transferring them to the adult system or handling them exclusively within the juvenile system, both of which present problems, states have begun exploring a third option: combining aspects of the juvenile and adult systems.

Youthful-offender or intermediate facilities allow states the option of placing in specialized hybrid settings serious offenders convicted in adult court or adjudicated delinquent in juvenile court. Like juvenile institutions, these facilities feature intensive counseling and treatment and avoid the risk of victimization by adult criminals; like adult prisons, they are secure and minimize the chance that juvenile inmates will victimize one another.

In 1993 Colorado set up a youthful-offender program whose primary goals are to eliminate gang ties and reduce violence. The program combines discipline, treatment, and reintegration into the community.

Wisconsin requires certain youthful offenders to remain in its program for five years or, if they have committed felonies that would be punishable by life imprisonment, until age 25. This allows the state to work with and closely monitor offenders during what are typically the most crime- and violence-prone years.

Other states have enacted laws providing for what is termed "blended sentencing." Essentially this means

Ages 13 to 14 are the peak years for juvenile property crimes. By contrast, violent criminality peaks around age 18. Supervision of juvenile offenders should take these facts into account, experts maintain.

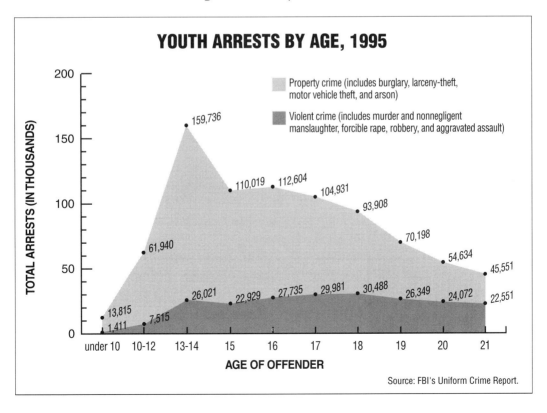

YOUTH ARRESTS BY AGE, 1995

Property crime (includes burglary, larceny-theft, motor vehicle theft, and arson)

Violent crime (includes murder and nonnegligent manslaughter, forcible rape, robbery, and aggravated assault)

TOTAL ARRESTS (IN THOUSANDS)

AGE OF OFFENDER

Source: FBI's Uniform Crime Report.

Restoring a sense of community may be the best way to prevent first-time and younger juvenile lawbreakers from developing into chronic offenders. Such is the rationale for programs like Youth Aid Panels, under which a child's case is removed from the juvenile justice system and handled by a group of specially trained private citizens. Resolutions are geared toward community service, such as cleaning up graffiti.

that a range of juvenile and adult sanctions may be used with certain offenders. Blended sentencing works differently in different states. In Minnesota serious and repeat juvenile offenders over 14 years old are classified as "extended sentence jurisdiction juveniles," and the juvenile justice system retains jurisdiction until they are 21, not 18 as is the customary age. If found guilty of a crime, extended sentence jurisdiction juveniles receive a juvenile disposition and a suspended criminal sentence. If they violate the terms of their juvenile disposition, they must serve the criminal sentence, which is usually a prison term.

In Florida criminal court judges may sentence an offender as a juvenile or as an adult. If the offender is sentenced as a juvenile, the judge retains jurisdiction, monitors compliance with the court order, and, if there is a violation, may resentence the offender as an adult.

Other states have enacted laws mandating the creation of an official, permanent record for certain serious, chronic, and violent offenders. This is designed to ensure that a crime committed after age 18, when a juvenile's records are typically sealed, isn't treated in criminal court as a first offense.

In still other states, blended sentencing means that juvenile courts have the power to impose long sentences that are served in both the juvenile and adult correctional systems. In Texas, for example, a juvenile found guilty of any of 12 violent felonies may be sentenced to 40 years in prison, beginning with treatment in a juvenile facility until age 18, at which time, after a court review, the juvenile may be transferred to an adult prison to serve out the rest of the sentence.

All of these innovative sentencing options are efforts to correct deficiencies in both the adult and juvenile justice systems—to treat juvenile offenders as humanely as possible while still protecting society, to give young lawbreakers a chance to turn away from a life of crime. A much better option, of course, is to reach children before they commit serious crimes in the first place. And that is precisely what community-based programs such as Youth Aid Panels are designed to do.

Youth Aid Panels, a relatively recent development in juvenile justice, are groups of citizens who have been trained by community dispute-settlement organizations to handle cases involving first-time offenders or juveniles who have committed status offenses or other minor crimes. A panel's task is to work out a resolution with the offender, his or her parents, and the victim (with whom they meet privately). Guilt and innocence are not at issue; rather, the resolution is geared toward having the juvenile make restitution for his or her offense. Possibilities range from repairing damage done through vandalism to community service work in a nursing home or firehouse. Instead of getting involved

Ultimately, the success of America's efforts to reduce juvenile crime may hinge less on law enforcement and punishment than on the nation's willingness to invest in its children.

with the juvenile justice system and being assigned a probation officer, the child gets involved with the community and, it is hoped, the community gets involved with the child.

Such connections could have far-reaching benefits. Not only might the individual offender have to confront, on a personal rather than an abstract level, the problems his or her actions have created for members of the community, but the community might come to understand better the problems its children face. And community ties, the disintegration of which is viewed as one of the causes of juvenile crime, might be built up once again.

According to the Coordinating Council on Juvenile Justice and Delinquency Prevention, programs such as the ones discussed above can and should play an integral role in a reinvigorated juvenile justice system that promotes "balanced and restorative justice" by achieving three key objectives: community protection, accountability, and competency development.

> Accountability refers to the requirement that juvenile offenders receive sanctions for their offenses and that they make amends to the victim and the community for harm caused. Competency development suggests that youth who enter the juvenile justice system should exit more capable of being productive, responsible citizens. Community protection requires that the juvenile justice system ensure public safety.

One more element that is currently being developed bears mentioning: intensive aftercare. After a juvenile has completed a treatment program or served a sentence in a correctional facility, ideally he or she would receive more monitoring and support than that provided by traditional parole arrangements. By working with family, peers, employers, and schools, aftercare programs might ease the offender's reintegration into the community and prepare him or her for progressive freedom and responsibility. One way this is being facilitated is by bringing probation officers into selected schools, where they can more easily monitor the behavior of at-risk juveniles; educate students, their families, and teachers about the juvenile justice system; work with school districts in combating truancy; and promptly defuse potential problems.

Ultimately, however, America's success in curbing juvenile crime might depend not so much on specific programs for punishing, rehabilitating, or supervising juvenile offenders but on our overall willingness to invest in the nation's youth. In the words of one probation official, "We have lost a generation of kids. *We've* done it, not the kids." And only by attacking the conditions that lead kids to crime—social ills such as poverty, violence, drug abuse, dysfunctional families, and failing schools—can the country truly protect its most precious resource: its children.

Further Reading

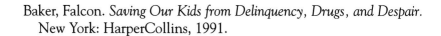

Baker, Falcon. *Saving Our Kids from Delinquency, Drugs, and Despair*. New York: HarperCollins, 1991.

Bing, Léon. *Do or Die*. New York: HarperCollins, 1991.

Coordinating Council on Juvenile Justice and Delinquency Prevention. *Combating Violence and Delinquency: The National Juvenile Justice Action Plan*. Washington, D.C.: Office of Juvenile Justice and Delinquency Prevention, 1996.

DiIulio, John J., Jr. "The Coming of the Super-Predators." *Weekly Standard*, November 27, 1995.

Hubner, John, and Jill Wolfson. *Somebody Else's Children: The Courts, the Kids, and the Struggle to Save America's Troubled Families*. New York: Crown Publishers, 1996.

Humes, Edward. *No Matter How Loud I Shout: A Year in the Life of Juvenile Court*. New York: Simon & Schuster, 1996.

Jones, Michael A., and Barry Krisberg. *Images and Reality: Juvenile Crime, Youth Violence, and Public Policy*. San Francisco: National Council on Crime and Delinquency, 1994.

Kozol, Jonathan. *Amazing Grace*. New York: Crown Publishers, 1995.

Lang, Susan S. *Teen Violence*. New York: Franklin Watts, 1991.

Platt, Anthony M. *Child Savers: The Invention of Delinquency*. 2nd ed. Chicago: University of Chicago Press, 1980.

Prescott, Peter S. *The Child Savers*. New York: Simon & Schuster, 1982.

Sikes, Gini. *8 Ball Chicks: A Year in the Violent World of Girl Gangsters*. New York: Doubleday, 1997.

Snyder, Howard N. *Juvenile Offenders and Victims: 1996 Update on Violence*. Washington, D.C.: Office of Juvenile Justice and Delinquency Prevention, 1996.

Snyder, Howard N., and Melissa Sickmund. *Juvenile Offenders and Victims: A National Report*. Washington, D.C.: Office of Juvenile Justice and Delinquency Prevention, 1995.

Index

MARCIA SATTERTHWAITE is a social worker and freelance writer. She lives near Philadelphia.

AUSTIN SARAT is William Nelson Cromwell Professor of Jurisprudence & Political Science at Amherst College, where he also chairs the Department of Law, Jurisprudence and Social Thought. Professor Sarat is the author or editor of 23 books and numerous scholarly articles. Among his books are *Law's Violence, Sitting in Judgment: Sentencing the White Collar Criminal,* and *Justice and Injustice in Law and Legal Theory.* He has received many academic awards and held several prestigious fellowships. In addition, he is a nationally recognized teacher and educator whose teaching has been featured in the *New York Times,* on the *Today* show, and on National Public Radio's *Fresh Air.*

Picture Credits